FRANCIS FRITH'S
PHOTOGRAPHIC MEMORIES

NORFOLK
A SECOND SELECTION

Popular East Anglian Writer BARRY PARDUE arrived in Norfolk some 40 years ago. Since then he has amassed considerable knowledge of the area. He is a regular contributor to the popular local radio station Radio Norfolk. He has written on various subjects such as advertising, engineering, marketing, training, and his favourite sport, golf.

Barry writes for various magazines, and is currently working on a series of books on events in Norfolk. He is also the author of *Francis Frith's Photographic Memories of King's Lynn*. This second selection of Norfolk, written in Barry's easy style, will prove fascinating and informative to everyone who has an interest in this beautiful County.

FRANCIS FRITH'S
PHOTOGRAPHIC MEMORIES

NORFOLK

A SECOND SELECTION

BARRY PARDUE

First published in the United Kingdom in 2003 by
Frith Book Company Ltd

Hardback Edition 2003
ISBN 1-85937-457-3

British Library Cataloguing in Publication Data

Francis Frith's Norfolk - A Second Selection
Barry Pardue

Frith Book Company Ltd
Frith's Barn, Teffont,
Salisbury, Wiltshire SP3 5QP
Tel: +44 (0) 1722 716 376
Email: info@francisfrith.co.uk
www.francisfrith.co.uk

Printed and bound in Great Britain

Front Cover: **GREAT YARMOUTH,** *Kings Street 1896* 37958

AS WITH ANY HISTORICAL DATABASE THE FRITH ARCHIVE IS CONSTANTLY BEING CORRECTED AND IMPROVED AND THE PUBLISHERS WOULD WELCOME INFORMATION ON OMISSIONS OR INACCURACIES

CONTENTS

FRANCIS FRITH

VICTORIAN PIONEER

FRANCIS FRITH, founder of the world-famous photographic archive, was a complex and multi-talented man. A devout Quaker and a highly successful Victorian businessman, he was philosophic by nature and pioneering in outlook.

By 1855 he had already established a wholesale grocery business in Liverpool, and sold it for the astonishing sum of £200,000, which is the equivalent today of over £15,000,000. Now a multi-millionaire, he was able to indulge his passion for travel. As a child he had pored over travel books written by early explorers, and his fancy and imagination had been stirred by family holidays to the sublime mountain regions of Wales and Scotland. 'What a land of spirit-stirring and enriching scenes and places!' he had written. He was to return to these scenes of grandeur in later years to 'recapture the thousands of vivid and tender memories', but with a different purpose. Now in his thirties, and captivated by the new science of photography, Frith set out on a series of pioneering journeys up the Nile and to the Near East that occupied him from 1856 until 1860.

INTRIGUE AND EXPLORATION

These far-flung journeys were packed with intrigue and adventure. In his life story, written when he was sixty-three, Frith tells of being held captive by bandits, and of fighting 'an awful midnight battle to the very point of surrender with a deadly pack of hungry, wild dogs'. Wearing flowing Arab costume, Frith arrived at Akaba by camel seventy years before Lawrence of Arabia, where he encountered 'desert princes and rival sheikhs, blazing with jewel-hilted swords'.

He was the first photographer to venture beyond the sixth cataract of the Nile. Africa was still the mysterious 'Dark Continent', and Stanley and Livingstone's historic meeting was a decade into the future. The conditions for picture taking confound belief. He laboured for hours in his wicker dark-room in the sweltering heat of the desert, while the volatile chemicals fizzed dangerously in their trays. Back in London he exhibited his photographs and was 'rapturously cheered' by members of the Royal Society. His reputation as a photographer was made overnight.

VENTURE OF A LIFE-TIME

Characteristically, Frith quickly spotted the opportunity to create a new business as a specialist publisher of photographs. He lived in an era of immense and sometimes violent change.

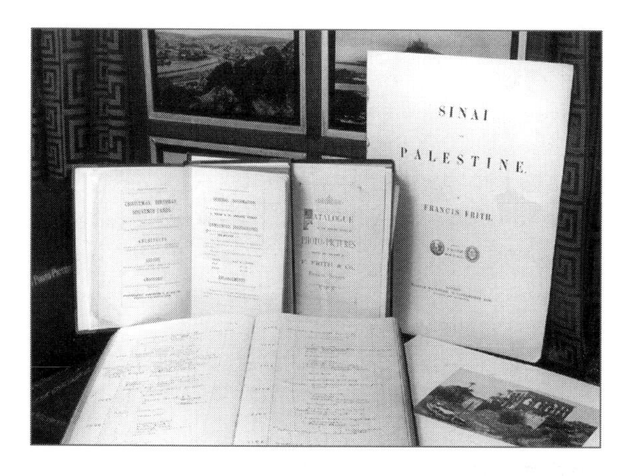

For the poor, in the early part of Victoria's reign, work was exhausting and the hours long, and people had precious little free time to enjoy themselves. Most had no transport other than a cart or gig at their disposal, and rarely travelled far beyond the boundaries of their own town or village. However, by the 1870s the railways had threaded their way across the country, and Bank Holidays and half-day Saturdays had been made obligatory by Act of Parliament. All of a sudden the working man and his family were able to enjoy days out and see a little more of the world.

With typical business acumen, Francis Frith foresaw that these new tourists would enjoy having souvenirs to commemorate their days out. In 1860 he married Mary Ann Rosling and set out on a new career: his aim was to photograph every city, town and village in Britain. For the next thirty years he travelled the country by train and by pony and trap, producing fine photographs of seaside resorts and beauty spots that were keenly bought by millions of Victorians. These prints were painstakingly pasted into family albums and pored over during the dark nights of winter, rekindling precious memories of summer excursions.

THE RISE OF FRITH & CO

Frith's studio was soon supplying retail shops all over the country. To meet the demand he gathered about him a small team of photographers, and published the work of independent artist-photographers of the calibre of Roger Fenton and Francis Bedford. In order to gain some understanding of the scale of Frith's business one only has to look at the catalogue issued by Frith & Co in 1886: it runs to some 670 pages, listing not only many thousands of views of the British Isles but also many photographs of most European countries, and China, Japan, the USA and Canada - note the sample page shown here from the hand-written Frith & Co ledgers recording the pictures. By 1890 Frith had created the greatest specialist photographic publishing company in the world, with over 2,000 sales outlets - more than the combined number that Boots and WH Smith have today! The picture on the next page shows the Frith & Co display board at Ingleton in the Yorkshire Dales. Beautifully constructed with mahogany frame and gilt inserts, it could display up to a dozen local scenes.

POSTCARD BONANZA

The ever-popular holiday postcard we know today took many years to develop. In 1870 the Post Office issued the first plain cards, with a pre-printed stamp on one face. In 1894 they allowed other publishers' cards to be sent through the mail with an attached adhesive halfpenny stamp. Demand grew rapidly, and in 1895 a new size of postcard was permitted called the court card, but there was little room for illustration. In 1899, a year after Frith's death, a new card measuring 5.5 x 3.5 inches became the standard format, but it was not until 1902 that the divided back came into being, so that the address and message could be on one face and a full-size illustration on the other. Frith & Co were in the vanguard of postcard development: Frith's sons Eustace and Cyril continued their father's monumental task, expanding the number of views offered to the public and recording more

St Catherine's College
Senate House & Library
Gerrard Hostel Bridge
Geological Museum
Addenbrooke's Hospital
St Mary's Church
Fitzwilliam Museum, Pitt Press &c
Buxton, The Crescent
The Colonnade
Public Gardens
Haddon Hall, View from the Terrace
Millers Dale

and more places in Britain, as the coasts and countryside were opened up to mass travel.

Francis Frith had died in 1898 at his villa in Cannes, his great project still growing. The archive he created continued in business for another seventy years. By 1970 it contained over a third of a million pictures showing 7,000 British towns and villages.

FRANCIS FRITH'S LEGACY

Frith's legacy to us today is of immense significance and value, for the magnificent archive of evocative photographs he created provides a unique record of change in the cities, towns and villages throughout Britain over a century and more. Frith and his fellow studio photographers revisited locations many times down the years to update their views, compiling for us an enthralling and colourful pageant of British life and character.

We are fortunate that Frith was dedicated to recording the minutiae of everyday life. For it is this sheer wealth of visual data, the painstaking chronicle of changes in dress, transport, street layouts, buildings, housing, engineering and landscape that captivates us so much today. His remarkable images offer us a powerful link with the past and with the lives of our ancestors.

THE VALUE OF THE ARCHIVE TODAY

Computers have now made it possible for Frith's many thousands of images to be accessed almost instantly. Frith's images are increasingly used as visual resources, by social historians, by researchers into genealogy and ancestry, by architects and town planners, and by teachers involved in local history projects.

In addition, the archive offers every one of us an opportunity to examine the places where we and our families have lived and worked down the years. Highly successful in Frith's own era, the archive is now, a century and more on, entering a new phase of popularity. Historians consider the Francis Frith Collection to be of prime national importance. It is the only archive of its kind remaining in private ownership. Francis Frith's archive is now housed in an historic timber barn in the beautiful village of Teffont in Wiltshire. Its founder would not recognize the archive office as it is today. In place of the many thousands of dusty boxes containing glass plate negatives and an all-pervading odour of photographic chemicals, there are now ranks of computer screens. He would be amazed to watch his images travelling round the world at unimaginable speeds through internet lines.

The archive's future is both bright and exciting. Francis Frith, with his unshakeable belief in making photographs available to the greatest number of people, would undoubtedly approve of what is being done today with his lifetime's work. His photographs depicting our shared past are now bringing pleasure and enlightenment to millions around the world a century and more after his death.

NORFOLK
AN INTRODUCTION

IT IS HARD to find Norfolk's equal when we consider its history, its wonderful countryside, its coastline, and its cities, towns and villages. Industries range from farming, fishing, food production and woollens to wooden products from its large expanses of forestry. The flat landscape, through which flow beautiful rivers and broads, is rich with all kinds of flora and fauna. The county abounds with legends and romantic stories, which are connected with the remains of its ancient castles and shrines.

Norfolk is the most eastern county of Britain, and has roughly 1.4 million acres of land. It is well known for a varied and highly cultivated soil - thanks to the loss of hedgerows, some of its vast plains of wheat and barley equal those of Canada and the USA. Indeed, Norfolk is known as 'the bread basket of England'. The north and east coasts face the North Sea, while to the west and south lie rivers such as the Great Ouse, the Welney, the Nene and the Waveney; the sea and the rivers make Norfolk a virtual island. The countryside in the north consists of quiet undulations which slope into pretty valleys. There are high cliffs at Hunstanton and Cromer. To the south are flat, well-drained marshes and fens. Huge forest plantations cover the Breckland area.

ACLE, *The Green from the Post Office c1926* A204004

The last serious battles in Norfolk were in the days of the Normans. In earlier times the Danes and the Angles regularly crossed swords; their remains are buried in the mounds still to be seen in the Thetford area. Here too there are barrows that are said to be even older, in which lie the remains of Boadicea, the queen of the Iceni, and her warriors, who died fighting the Romans. Older still are Grimes Graves at Brandon: in fact, these are not graves at all, but Stone Age mines where axes and arrowheads and other weapons were created out of Norfolk flint. Flint is an attractive and everlasting building material that can be seen throughout Norfolk - it is used to build churches, manors, guildhalls, houses and walls. The stone is still worked today by flint knappers in the same way that it was in the Stone Age.

Norfolk was the nearest landing point for invaders from across the North Sea. Yarmouth was used many times by the Saxons, Danes and Gallic Celts. All over the county it is possible to see the remains of Roman encampments and roads. Coins and treasures are still being found by local and visiting treasure hunters with their metal detectors. Pilgrims and traders created well-worn tracks on their way to the Chapel of our Lady of Walsingham, which is almost as popular with pilgrims as Lourdes in France. Norfolk is now relatively hard to get to by road from the rest of the country. Its airport needs enlarging, and apart from King's Lynn most ports are mainly concerned with fishing and servicing oil and gas rigs off the coast. The railways are still not as convenient as they might be.

Castles and castellated halls abound, mainly built by the Normans; there are excellent examples at Norwich, Castle Acre and Castle Rising, and also at Middleton near Lynn and Caistor Hall near Yarmouth. Some of these fine buildings are composed of iron-coloured carr-stone, which is probably the only building stone, apart from flint, that is quarried locally.

The attitude of some Norfolk people can be likened to those inhabiting a small island. The county is noted as being one of the most suspicious areas of England. It was once said that while Yorkshire and Lancashire men 'thump you on the back in a friendly fashion', in Norfolk they look as though they will hit you on the head - until they size you up. It is also said that one Norfolk farmer could beat any three Yorkshiremen in driving a bargain. The harsh history of different invaders has left its mark: visitors to the county should never become annoyed or take Norfolk humour the wrong way, remembering that it derives from bad experiences in ancient times. There is an old joke about a visiting Viking who had just come ashore from a long boat. He spotted a local and said: 'Good morning, bor! Which is the way to the church?' 'What d'ye want to know for?' retorted the Norfolk man. 'Well', said the Viking, 'we thought about setting fire to it'! (If you are addressed as 'bor' - the word comes from 'neighbour' - you can consider yourself as being accepted.)

Burnham Market is a favoured spot for the second homes of Londoners, who have created high property prices. Apart from this, the county has remained off the list of those tourists who like to flash in and out of towns and cities with no time to stop and appreciate local history. Norfolk people are quite happy to let them continue to visit London, Bath, Stratford on Avon, Edinburgh and the like. However, visitors will get a warm welcome whenever they do arrive.

Norwich itself could only be a Norfolk city; it would not fit comfortably in another county or country. It was once the third most important city in England, whose wealth was based on the weaving and shoe-making trade. Many fine medieval streets and buildings have been retained, a number of which show Dutch and Flemish influences with huge top stories where hand-looms were housed.

Norwich includes some villages which still retain their old names and parish churches, such as St John's Timberhill and St Miles Coslany. There are relics of the Neolithic and Bronze Ages here, together with Roman artefacts. Norwich Castle was built after the Norman conquest on top of an enlarged natural mound which existed before the 11th century. Henry III came to Norwich in the 12th century to settle arguments between the citizens and the Benedictine priory following the control of the castle by Louis, the French Dauphin. The Flemish weavers established a tremendous trade in the city during the 13th century, which spread from Norwich throughout the county.

Two peasant uprisings took place in Norwich: the first was in 1381, and the second nearly two hundred years later in 1549. It was headed by Robert Kett, a tanner from Wymondham. A strong force, (including many German mercenaries) led by the Earl of Warwick, suppressed the rebellion on Mousehold Heath (just outside the city). Kett was hung from the wall of the castle.

In the 16th century Queen Elizabeth visited the city for a week, staying at the Bishop's Palace. Apart from pageants and shows, the Queen spent most of her time hunting in Costessey Park.

The beautiful Norwich Cathedral was started in 1096, and over hundreds of years was enlarged, altered, and damaged by several fires, some lit by the citizens. The monastic cloister is the largest in England. The boundaries of the cathedral and the Bishop's Palace are by the riverside, where there is a picturesque watergate known as Pulls Ferry; it is featured on countless calendars and paintings.

A separate book could be written about the rivalry of Yarmouth and Lowestoft, both extremely important ports. Crossing over Yarmouth's Haven Bridge we cannot miss the spire of one of the largest parish churches in England. We can also see the famous Star Hotel, which was originally the home of William Crowe; its rich ornamentation was designed to display his enormous wealth. Nelson is said to have stayed there after he landed at Yarmouth following the victory at the Battle of the Nile. He was made a freeman of the borough, and when he died at Trafalgar, the town erected a lofty monument to his memory.

Along Yarmouth's South Quay there are a few old flint-faced buildings, but many of the buildings show a strong continental influence - in fact, the narrow rows remind one of Amsterdam. Even Dickens's David Copperfield noticed the Dutch influence; like Holland, Yarmouth was taken from the sea, which periodically tries to take it back by disastrous flooding. In the 18th century, Dutch and Yarmouth fishermen were extremely friendly, and at one time 'Dutch Sunday' (the first Sunday before 21 September) was observed in the town with a ceremony called 'wetting the nets'. People from all over Norfolk came to see the many and varied celebrations. Dutch and local dignitaries wore their most flamboyant uniforms and robes, and the townsfolk and visitors wore their Sunday best clothes. There are few very old buildings left: just the fishermen's almshouses, and the Tollhouse, which could be the oldest municipal building in England. Visitors to Yarmouth who prefer only to be entertained by the theatres, side-shows and amusements miss a tremendous amount if they fail to look back into the town's history.

The origin of the Broads lies back in early medieval times. At the time when monastic houses were being founded throughout Norfolk from Bungay to Acle and beyond, the chosen sites for these were always close to rivers and marshes, which were full of fowl and fish to sustain the monks, nuns and baronial families. This was the time when the first efforts were being made to drain and embank these wetlands, which also provided the perfect habitat for birds of every description and breed.

In the 13th century there was a successful effort by the sea to reclaim its lost ground during a violent storm. The sea rushed into towns and villages, crushing houses, and drowning people, animals and crops. This tragedy repeated itself centuries later in 1607; the sea created havoc along the coast into Suffolk, Essex and Kent, killing many thousands of people. (Bad though this sounds, the plague or black death was worse: it killed nearly sixty thousand during 1349 in Norwich and Yarmouth alone.)

The wherrymen were the prime movers of grain, coal, timber, harvested reeds, crops and manufactured goods throughout Broadland and to the coastal ports - their trade continued even when the railways arrived. In the 17th century a new chain of waterways was cut, which connected many broads. This is when the Broads were discovered by holidaymakers. They came in small numbers to start with, because accommodation

WELLS-NEXT-THE-SEA, *The Quay c1955* W48064

was limited to the pubs and inns close to the waterways, and the yachts and boats in use at that time had little or no living space. The reputation of the Broads spread throughout the country, mainly because of its wildlife and its unique landscape. Local entrepreneurs soon grasped the opportunity to provide craft now equipped with every creature comfort and suitably designed to cope with the shallow water.

The true beauty of the area however, even now, can only be seen at its best if one is prepared to walk the river banks where it is impossible to sail or navigate cruisers. Only then is the scenery, and the bonus of meeting inhabitants both human and animal, fully appreciated. Most marshlands are aptly called wild-flower gardens. Some contain rare species and floral treasures, including grasses and sedges which are found nowhere else apart from Norfolk. Nature has a way of preserving its rare plants by growing them in the most inaccessible places, usually unclaimed swamps; this is where local knowledge is critical, and it is essential to befriend a local fenman if you want to find special varieties, and to keep yourself safe and dry on the dykes and fens. Unfortunately, to meet the men who have spent their lives on the Broads is not as easy as it sounds. After all, with today's conservation policies they are not allowed to take fish and wild birds, so they cannot make a living in the same way that their ancestors did.

There is no doubt that the Broads is the most popular and well known part of Norfolk, because of the popularity of holidays afloat. The pressure of this type of holiday has taken its toll on the wildlife, and occasionally arguments do take place between fishermen and sailors. These are usually caused by boats exceeding the laid-down speed restrictions, which creates bank damage and also pollution. Nevertheless, there are still species of plants unique to Broadland, and Norfolk reed is still the best material for thatching. The Broads are of value to the whole country, not just Norfolk. It is vital that their continued welfare is monitored from the highest level, with government funding if necessary, to ensure that conservationists from all interested parties can maintain their vigilance.

If you like to travel to see beautiful things, then this county cannot be beaten for its noble churches, attractive buildings, and beautiful scenery. It is difficult to find the words to convey the charm and character of Norfolk and its people, but the rewards when you get to know them leaves an imperishable memory.

THE BROADS, *The Pool, Wayford Bridge c1945* T213065

NORWICH AND DISTRICT

NORWICH
Westlegate Street 1890 24044

All Saints' church stands like a watchtower over this street, which houses many small businesses. Norwich is known as 'the City of Churches', and All Saints' is one of forty; it has an ancient font finely carved with figures of saints and the twelve apostles. The great plague of 1349 virtually depopulated this area of the city, so that the church incorporated the benefice of nearby St Catherine's, Newgate. Noah Shalders was the pawnbroker on the right-hand side of this cobbled street - he was not known for his generosity.

BUNTING
& WOOLLEN

NORWICH
Rampant Horse Street 1891 28163

Not visible in this photograph, but well worth walking to see at the west end of the street, is St Stephen's church, a large and handsome building which was founded before the Norman Conquest. Colman the cutler and ironmonger (right) was a partner of Glendenning, a saddler and travelling case maker for the gentry. Arthur Bunting (left) dealt in woollens and linen; Curl Brothers owned the huge shop on the right of the picture, which was floodlit at night by the eight lamp posts erected on the pavement. Curls was a popular forerunner of today's department stores.

NORWICH
The Cattle Market and the Castle 1891 28177

The dignified square castle dominates the city from its prehistoric mound. In 1345 it became the county gaol, and for the most part was not to play a great role in the county's history. It now houses a splendid museum. Huge sheep markets were held here, and the farmers and buyers refreshed themselves in the Woolpack, a convenient public house across the road from the castle.

NORWICH
Stranger's Hall 1919 69049

Now a museum and well preserved, this ancient building was a 15th-century merchant's house, and was also owned in its history by two Norwich mayors. It is a fascinating building, with 16th-century flint work and a timber-framed jettied first floor. The building contains examples of domestic furniture along with maps and illustrations of old Norwich.

▲ **NORWICH,** *The Post Office and Prince of Wales Road 1896* 37362

This photograph is elegant in every way, from the smartly dressed family in the foreground (who are in need of a pushchair or pram), to the pony and traps and elegant Georgian and Victorian buildings. The post office on the right was formerly the Agricultural Hall. At the Royal Hotel on the left the author first sampled samphire, a Norfolk delicacy found growing in salt marshes around the coast. This has become so popular that you need a licence to pick it.

◄ **TAVERHAM**
Taverham Hall c1960
T212004

This attractive three-storey building is in the Jacobean and Tudor style much favoured by its builder, David Brandon. On the right, note the interesting polygonal turret finishing in a gable which blends nicely into the roof. It was an early home of the Micklethwait family, and has been a school since the 1920s.

▼ **LODDON,** *Chedgrave Basin c1965* L369011

This small market town is on the River Chet; even these moored boats and yachts would have had difficulty in navigating this shallow tributary of the River Yare to get to the pleasant town centre. There are varied shops, good pubs and a fine church housing old paintings of the Hobart family and of the builder who constructed the church in 1496.

▲ **BRUNDALL**
On the Yare c1960 B497001

An old family from Saint Omer were lords of this village. Under Henry VII it was given to the Hobarts for several generations. This is a popular spot on the Yare to start and finish a Broads holiday, or merely to top up with fuel for both body and boat; Note the signs for Lyons cakes and Walls ice cream (left), which in their day were as recognisable as Big Macs. Here you can moor the boat and enjoy some of the best coarse fishing in the country. There used to be a wild fowl decoy, as there was plentiful bird life here; but the noise from the boatyards has tended to frighten the birds away.

AROUND THE BROADS

THE BROADS *1902* 48171

Norfolk folk were sailing on the winding, slow-flowing rivers and angling and wild fowling on the Broads well before holidaymakers from outside the area discovered its virtues in the late 1870s. The sailors in the picture appear to be trying to rescue a stray pig, although they have nearly run aground in doing so. He could prove to be an unwelcome passenger.

THE BROADS
A Greengrocer on the Broads c1945
T213029

Farmers' markets are not only held in villages! These enterprising retailers are taking advantage of a captive market on the Broads. This floating shop is more than welcome with holidaymakers, who are not keen to lose sailing time by visiting shops on land. They also enjoy a 'mardle', or bargain, and barter for a good deal.

THE BROADS, *Yachting on the Broads c1960* T213092

Salt water is not required in your veins to appreciate the pleasure of navigating the region in this typical Broads sailing cruiser, shown here in full sail. Unlike motorised cruisers, these flat-bottomed boats do not cause bank damage, which can be created by wash from excessive speeds or pollution from engine fuel, both of which are kept under control by the authorities.

THE BROADS, *Home at Evening c1900* T213078

What a blissful way to get home at the end of the day. Imagine the pleasure of gliding along between meadow grass and wild flowers on the banks, accompanied by the music of birdsong. We can only envy the lady in this picturesque scene of Norfolk Broads tranquillity.

THE BROADS *The 'Silver Swallow' c1945* T213349

This beautifully-designed broads cruiser is typical of those provided by the holiday companies, who have already expanded into huge businesses. By using power and not sail, it is possible to make the most of valuable holiday time to explore a large area of the Broads while living in comfort.

REEDHAM, *The Orphanage 1903* 49455

This small town stands on a inlet of the River Wensum. Lothbroc, a Danish king, landed at Reedham in an open boat when he was driven ashore during a violent storm. Built in the Elizabethan style, the orphanage has room for one hundred children.

REEDHAM
The Beauchamp Arms Hotel c1955 R303303

Rising outside Norwich, the Yare flows 25 miles from the city to Yarmouth; all of this stretch is navigable by river craft - Roman war-galleys sailed right up to Norwich. The stately broads sailing boats are available to hire outside the Beauchamp Arms Hotel, which is situated in a perfect location for tourists, whether they are sailors or not. Reedham has the highest windpump in Norfolk: it is 70ft high and was built in 1870.

THE BROADS
On The Waveny 1902
48138

This area is not as popular with most holidaymakers as the areas around the rivers Yare or Bure. But sailors appreciate the scenery here, which is equal to any landscape painted by Constable. Village lanes and woodlands can be discovered and explored within a short distance from many moorings on the river Waveney, which separates Norfolk from Suffolk.

REEDHAM
The Ferry c1955
R303300

This ferry leaves from the Ferry Inn, where the passengers from this coach are probably still enjoying their Guinness or local ale. Although Sutton's coaches came up from Clacton on Sea, no doubt the scenery and wildlife is an attractive contrast to candy floss, deckchairs and the beach.

CANTLEY
The Red House Hotel c1965 C414008

Although it is close to the sugar-processing factory, this village on the River Yare is an ideal spot for holidaymakers. The mooring is free, the meals at the hotel are good, and there is a ferry and a railway by which you can travel to Norwich, Lowestoft and Yarmouth quicker than by boat; no wonder Cantley is popular with visitors and locals alike.

ACLE
The Green from the Post Office c1926
A204004

Every possible mode of transport can be seen at the junction on the A47 main road to Yarmouth from Norwich. Acle is a busy market town, one of the early possessions of the Bigods, who founded a priory here during the reign of Edward I. Acle has one of the biggest livestock markets in the county, especially for pigs - some families keep one or two pigs in their backyards for their own use and resale. This practice, which originated because of the shortage of meat after the First World War, has been retained today.

ACLE
The Staithe c1929
A204005

Acle is a popular centre for amateur yachtsmen, who come ashore to explore the area and visit the inns used by local rivermen. These robust characters earn their living all year round on dark-sailed wherries, which are dingier than the white-hulled craft we see here, including the large broads holiday cruiser.

ACLE, *The 17th-Century Windmill c1929* A204048

The sails on the pleasure dinghy are as worn as those on the ancient windmill standing out boldly on the edge of the river. The windmill is characteristic of this area, which attracts tourists and naturalists from all over Britain.

SOUTH WALSHAM
The Churches 1934
86385

Two churches in one churchyard is very unusual. St Laurence's was destroyed by fire in 1827, but its ivy-covered tower remains. The replacement church of St Mary has attractive carved figures in its porch; inside there is a fine oak chest and an inscribed oak screen. The pews have carved poppy-heads with the donor's initials.

RANWORTH, *Reed Stacks c1955* R9001

Reeds reach their full height in autumn, so reed cutting and stacking is done early in the next year so that the reeds dry throughout the summer. This is a characteristic scene: the reeds are stacked alongside old farmhouses and cottages waiting to be taken away by wide flat-bottomed craft such as wherries and barges. The beautiful bull-nosed touring car looks as if it could go in both directions at the same time!

HORNING
The Village 1902 48106

This is a pretty scene with a handsome ash tree in the background, and two children in a quiet side street. Horning's legendary Benedictine abbey was destroyed by invaders, rebuilt in splendour by kings, and was not suppressed by Henry VIII. All this seems miles away from the activities on the Broad, which is just around the corner.

THE BROADS
Horning Broad 1902 48140

The flat landscape of the Broads is broken by windmills, church towers, or the masts of sailing boats. This area is a haven for all wildlife, but it is also a favourite haunt for flight-shooters who have taken many rare birds; some of which are on display in Norwich museum. At times the local Inns were kept busy with as many gunners as anglers. The Ferry Inn used to have a splendid male Bittern shot by the landlord; this breed of bird has now virtually disappeared from Broadland.

HORNING
The Ferry 1921
70902

Boats moored here are hired out by the owner of the Ferry Inn. The horse-drawn ferry has a history going back to the 13th century. This reed-fringed part of the Bure and its riverside inn is typical of Broadland.

◀ **HORNING**
The Village 1921
70904

It is lunch time in the village; the post office is closed, and the lady street vendor is resting on her cart. Advertising signs show two makes of chocolate, but Caley's is the brand manufactured in Norfolk and favoured by the locals.

▼ **HORNING,** *On the Broad 1934* 86374

This typical Broad scene shows sailing and fishing going on, with a wind-pump in the background. At this time sailing boats predominated over motorised cruisers; the Broads were quieter and more tranquil as a result.

► **WROXHAM**
The Broad 1902 48132

This broad is almost a mile long, and at this part of it the dinghy passengers and the cattle are enjoying a quiet moment. The water is as smooth as glass, and the varied trees, the aquatic plants at the water's edge, and the reeds in the distance are a complete contrast to what goes on further down the broad at Wroxham bridge. Here there are fleets of cruisers, pleasure boats, racers, and even the wherries. Their crews or passengers arrive by car, coach or train, and the atmosphere is of gaiety and revelry with dialects from all corners of the country, and the sound of music from guitars, accordions and even banjos.

WROXHAM
Station Road 1921
70891

Once a small village, Wroxham has now grown large as a result of the number of people intent on a cruising holiday. Local businesses have flourished. In Station Road you can book a motorboat or cruiser, and if you are a land-lubber or onlooker you could enjoy a meal in one of the many restaurants.

WROXHAM
The River Bure 1921
70892

One of the three main rivers which drain the Broads, the Bure is typically slow-flowing; a large number of cruising boats from Collins & Son (in the background) confine their cruising to the River Bure. The four cygnets in their grey plumage are being protected by their parents. On the far bank is an attractive thatched waterside summer-house which also acts as a boathouse.

COLTISHALL
The River 1902 48114

On the River Bure, Coltishall is a picturesque place and an important centre for building the famous Norfolk wherry. Thomas Wright was a well-known boat builder, and so were Allen's, who considered their designs to be the quickest on the Broads. The height of the mast can clearly be seen on the moored wherry on the right of the picture; it would have to be laid flat to negotiate the many low road bridges on the Broads.

COLTISHALL
The Lock 1902 48123

This pretty river between Coltishall and Aylsham has three locks and seven bridges, creating quite a bit of work for the boat crews. This is perhaps too much work for some holidaymakers, who tend to prefer the larger and more open Broads.

COLTISHALL
The Mill 1902 48148

This fine old building houses a large water-mill, which like most of Norfolk's water-mills has a hidden undershot wheel. This design is used because the Norfolk rivers are not powerful enough to work an overshot wheel. Traditional wherries were able to dock at the mill to collect its grain and flour. The villagers of Coltishall were favoured by Henry III: the local lords of the manor could not order the locals to do anything, or dispose of them, settle their quarrels or disputes or force them into villeinage. Once a year, under the direct authority of the King, his officers sorted out the villagers' problems.

HORSTEAD
The Mill 1934 86399

This water-mill, powered by a hidden undershot wheel, stands on the bank of the river Bure, and is built of entirely of wood. There are two large millstones leaning on the small annexe. The diagonal chute pours milled grain straight into barges and wherries. This picturesque view has been painted by many artists, and is considered equal to Constable's Flatford on the Stour.

BELAUGH, *The Church 1921* 70897

'Belaugh' means 'the dwelling-place at the water'. The church is in a commanding position 75 yards from the water's edge, which at one time covered all the land at its base, even where the cottages in the picture have been built. The bottom of the church steeple is higher than the roof of the parsonage, just visible in the trees. At one time the churchyard wall decayed, rainwater washed the soil away from the graves, and bones were taken down the hill, even into the water. The lords of the manor, who took their name from the village, came here in the time of Henry II; John, son of Ybri de Belaugh, had a large estate.

NEATISHEAD, *Barton Broad c1940* N136001

These boats are moored in a small creek off the wide waters of the broad. The pleasure craft in the foreground has a steering wheel which would not be out of place in a bus or taxi.

THE BROADS, *Yachting on the River Ant c1955* T213027

There is not a breath of wind, so the drainage mill is motionless and the sailing boats are becalmed on the Ant, which is little more than a narrow stream at this point. The river is so shallow that only small flat-bottomed boats or gun-punts can navigate its channels, and sailors spend more time tacking from side to side than moving in a straight line. This area is a haven for voles and water-fowl.

THE BROADS, *The Pool, Wayford Bridge c1945* T213065

This bridge is owned by the Drainage Commissioners, and has been rebuilt to give the river two feet more room. The height above water level has been kept the same to maintain this point of the River Ant as the navigational limit. The boat is essential to the cottage owner, and so are long wellingtons, because his property has been flooded on numerous occasions.

▼ **THE BROADS,** *On Ludham Broad c1945* T213007

Both the house and lodge are roofed in local Norfolk reed, known throughout the land as the best material for this purpose. Most houses alongside the Broads have boathouses rather than garages, and are ideally situated and sought-after as idyllic retreats for authors and writers as well as for local people.

► **LUDHAM**
The Village 1934 86375

This pretty village has a number of attractive houses. This picture shows the varied building materials used in Norfolk: flint, clay-lump and the famous Norfolk Red brick. In the centre stand good examples of cottages thatched with Norfolk reed, and beyond are roof pantiles brought over by the Dutch. The village store has a good range of gardening tools on display.

THE BROADS, *St Bennet's Abbey 1934* 86380

This abbey was founded by Canute in the year 1020. The ruins make it hard to believe in its history of royal visits; on one of these, the mayor of Norwich arrived with a hundred citizens to present a petition to the king's mother in 1469. The abbot of St Bennet's had a seat in the House of Lords. The drainage mill was erected over a magnificent gateway to the abbey, which looked more like a castle than a cloister.

LUDHAM *The Mills 1934* 86377A

Norfolk is full of windmills - there used to be one on every piece of elevated land. Apart from milling, they were used to drain the fens and broads; their numbers dropped when fuel-powered engines were introduced. Ludham has an example of the oldest type of hollow-post wind-pump, which is around three hundred years old.

▼ POTTER HEIGHAM, *The Windmill c1926* P167008

This type of elegant windmill came into its own during the spring and autumn when the marshes were often full of flood water; during this time it was literally 'all hands to the pump' to ensure the safety of the cattle who had been turned out onto the land.

▲ **POTTER HEIGHAM**
The River Thurne 1934 86382

Typical sailing cruisers glide majestically along the River Thurne, passing one of the essential wind pumps which drain the fields throughout the Broads area.

▼ **POTTER HEIGHAM,** *The Bridge Hotel c1955* P167047

There are some old paintings of the 14th-century bridge at Potter Heigham, which was a favourite subject with artists. This hotel serves the tourists who come to this popular boating centre.

► **POTTER HEIGHAM**
The River Thurne c1926 P167052

There are boats of every description on this busy part of the river. If the crew had not lowered the mast of the boat in the foreground, the 14th-century bridge with a headroom of only 7ft would have done the job for them.

◀ **HICKLING**
The Pleasure Boat Inn c1955 H307010

The young coxswain in the skiff has misjudged her three-point turn, and is wedged between the quayside and the cruiser. Because of the many dykes and staithes around the edges of the Broad, small sailing boats are the handiest for exploration.

▶ **HICKLING**
The Pleasure Boat Inn c1955 T213059

Close to Hickling Green and Norfolk's largest stretch of water, Hickling Broad, this pub is the start and welcoming finishing point for holidaymakers, walkers and naturalists. This is where the Broads become quite shallow. The area is so popular that in order to protect and preserve it, it is likely to become a national nature reserve.

ORMESBY
The Jetty 1887 19877

Ormesby probably derived its name from the Norse 'orm', a favourite ship's name of the Vikings, meaning 'sea serpent'. Although the Broad is well wooded, this is a typical quiet creek, fringed with reed, fen sedge, and a multitude of plants which attract birds, butterflies and insects. In the winter, it is a favourite visiting-place for wild-fowl, and it is popular in the season for fishermen.

ORMESBY
The Sportsman's Arms c1955 O78007

Villagers bound for a day trip to Great Yarmouth are being collected by coach outside the pub. Ormesby was once an important market town whose inhabitants were privileged to be exempt from county service, and from contributing funds towards the maintenance of the Shire Knights. No such luck today - they have to conform like the rest of us.

GREAT YARMOUTH AND THE EAST COAST

GORLESTON
The Pier 1908 60662

As it points Eastwards towards the North Sea where most of the stormy winds come from, there are not many occasions when visitors or locals can take advantage of the shelter on this pier. It was substantially built of concrete, stone and oak to defend this part of the harbour from the mountainous seas which pound the Norfolk coast. Passengers are waiting for the incoming pleasure steamer. The pier is a favourite spot for anglers.

GORLESTON
The White Lion Hotel 1922 72546

This is still one of Gorleston's most popular hotels, and nicely situated at the top of Cliff Hill. In this picture, guests are returning from the beach and are processing up to the hotel in order to get changed in time for their evening meal, which was often accompanied by soothing live music.

GREAT YARMOUTH, *The Fishermen's Hospital 1896* 19896

The old gentlemen on the right is a typical resident of the hospital, more so than the smart gentleman on the left, strolling with a lady who is keeping up with the latest fashion of a bustled skirt. The hospital was founded in 1702; it could accommodate up to twenty fishermen, who were either disabled or over 60 years old. In the background is the spire of St Nicholas's church.

GREAT YARMOUTH *Trafalgar Terrace 1887* 19870

More prosperous-looking than Yarmouth's famous narrow Rows, this spacious terrace is not the home of the working population, but of the more middle class. Residents here have their own pony and traps, including miniature vehicles and ponies for their children.

GREAT YARMOUTH, *The Fish Market c1900* G56503

After a good fishing trip, the drifters have unloaded their haul into baskets known as swills. Here on the wharf the tellers (in bowler hats) would assess the catch prior to its sale by auction. A high proportion of the catch would be herring, which would be gutted by hundreds of Scots fisher girls; the fish would then be dried and cured into the famous Great Yarmouth kippers.

FINE WINES
FROM THE
WOOD
AT
WHOLESALE
PRICES
REGENT
STREET
42

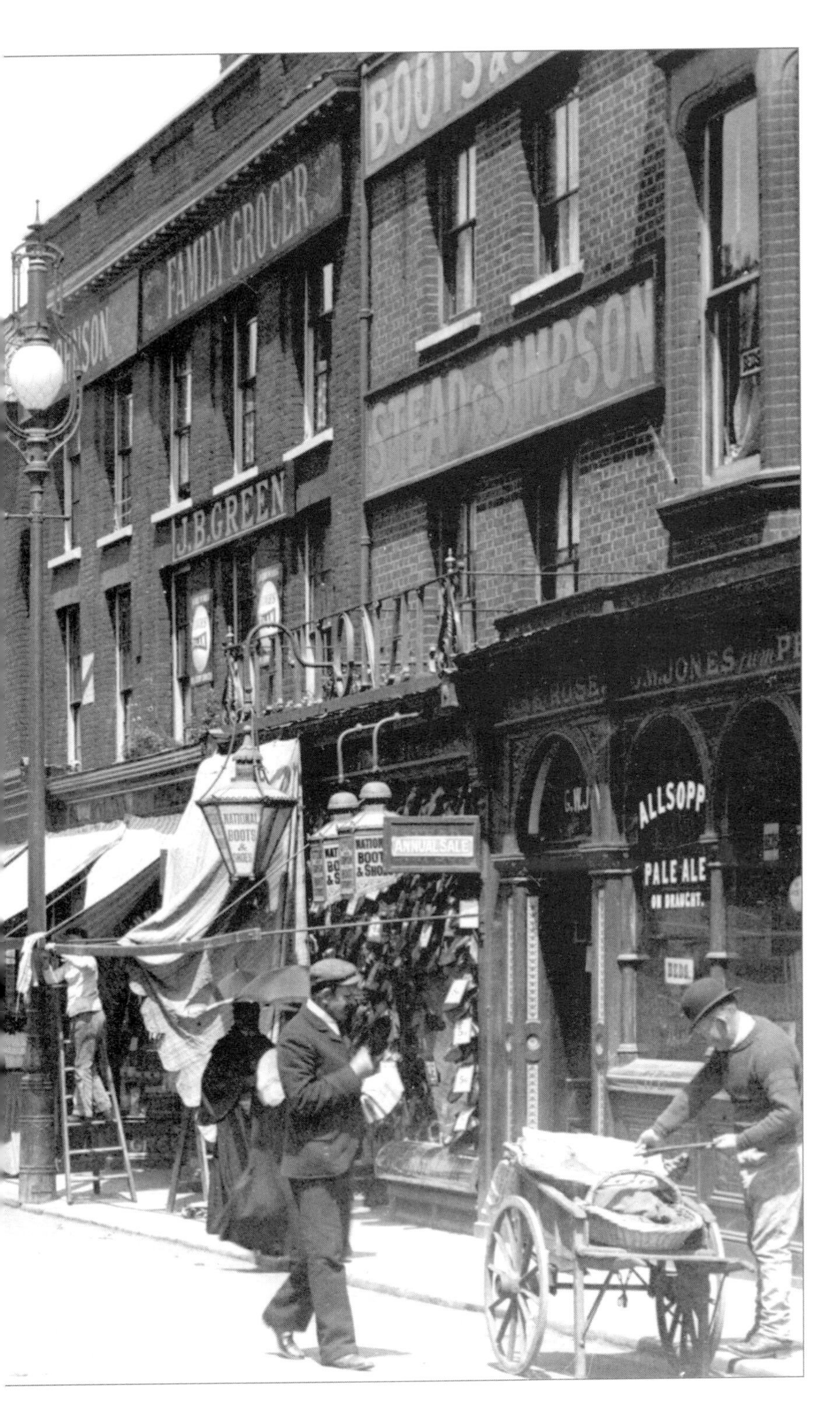

GREAT YARMOUTH
Kings Street 1896 37958

This is the busiest and main shopping street in Great Yarmouth. Everything is available here, from wine (left) to shoes (right). The family-owned businesses are thriving with the absence of department stores. Most of the attractive lamp-posts are used for advertising. The policeman in the foreground is casting a watchful and perhaps thirsty eye on the wine barrels being transported slowly up the street.
A number of superstitious people are avoiding walking under the window cleaners' ladders on the left and right.

▲ **GREAT YARMOUTH**
The Royal Aquarium 1895 37951

Originally the Royalty, this building was a leisure complex in 1875, with a skating rink, aquarium, bars and restaurants. A huge budget of £50,000 was provided for the building, but only half was used, and it was never completed. It opened as an aquarium in 1883, but this was also unsuccessful; today it is a cinema. The façade is constructed in gault brick from Costessey, a village just outside Norwich.

► **CAISTER-ON-SEA**
The Lifeboat Monument 1908 60671

This impressive memorial commemorates the deaths of nine crewmen who lost their lives when the lifeboat 'Beauchamp' capsized on 14 November 1901. The middle headstone on the left is for the late coxswain James Haylett, who had pulled the only two survivors out of the water. The Caister lifeboat is no longer under the RNLI, and relies totally on local fund raising. However, the comedian Jim Davidson is a keen supporter of this lifeboat, and has had the crew on his TV programme in an effort to give them well-deserved publicity.

CAISTER-ON-SEA, *The Castle 1908* 60665

Built from English bricks which were transported to Caister by sea, this castle dates from the time of Henry VI. In 1449 it belonged to Sir John Falstolf. The castle underwent a great siege, which went on for over a year until the 3,000 occupants were weakened by hunger and lack of gunpowder for their weapons. The siege finally collapsed, and the king transferred the castle to the Paston family, whose 15th-century letters are world-famous. The hollow circular tower is open to the elements, and provides a good home for hundreds of pigeons. It is over 100ft high, and is divided into four storeys. It is connected to a dining parlour 60ft long and 28ft wide - the remains of its fireplace can still be seen. The man in the skiff is floating on the tranquil moat, which is said to have once been connected to the Yare and then the North Sea. In the shadow of the tower, picnickers on the grass can relax and dream of centuries past.

THE NORTH EAST

BOOTON
The Church c1965 B539001

The architect and builders clearly enjoyed themselves using typical Norfolk materials: split flint work and ornate roof tiles. The details on the towers are particularly remarkable. This is a comparatively modern building - it was built between 1875 and 1900 by the Rev Whitewell Elwin.

CAWSTON
High Street c1965 C415010

In its heyday this was a huge village with shops of every description and five prosperous inns; there was even a beer house run by Matthew Austin. Different businesses produced hats, dresses, watches and clocks; a team of rat-catchers came from the village, and were well-known across the county. D Cook (right) is an electrical engineer - in the 1800s, Martha Cook was a well-known dressmaker. The fine church has a 120ft-high tower; it is famous for its hammer-beam roof and fine rood-screen. Centuries ago the pulpit had a large leather funnel with a pipe going down to a pew for a particularly deaf member of the congregation.

AYLSHAM, *Market Place c1955* A220023

Aylsham is a pleasant market town steeped in the history of woollen manufacture. Back in the days of Edward II, it was the principal town in the region for making fine linen. Its products were shipped to Yarmouth on barges capable of carrying several tonnes of material. This picture was taken just before shop closing time, for it looks unusually quiet. Some fine buildings stand in this part of the town centre; there are many other good ones - the Black Boys Inn and the Old Hall are the best examples. The locals say that Diane's snacks (left) were tastier than any burger or hot-dog available today.

▼ BARNINGHAM HALL *1922* 72673

Barningham Hall was built by Sir William Paston in about 1612. This view of the entrance front shows an excellent example of Jacobean work. The local church has a tablet and hatchments to the Paston family, and also a brass to John Winter, who was an MP for Norfolk in 1409.

► ALDBOROUGH

The Village c1955 A278007

Fine 'Norfolk Red' brick-and-flint work is evident on all the buildings. The postman (centre) has probably purchased some parts from Fisher's, who sell all the top brands of bicycles - not that the GPO buy top-of-the-range transport for their rural postmen! The shop is advertising brands which are no longer in existence apart from Raleigh. The Black Boys has been a popular inn for over 100 years; behind its signpost is a fine Zephyr, one of Ford's first vehicles with independent front suspension and column gear-change.

THORPE MARKET
The Tower, Gunton Park c1955
T256018

The whole of Gunton village is included in the park and grounds of Gunton Hall. There are lakes and extensive woodlands in the park, and also an old oak tree whose height is 42ft and whose girth is 21ft 6ins. The road from Thorpe passes under this stately tower: it is 120ft high, and commands a wonderful view over the surrounding area.

THORPE MARKET
Gunton Hall c1955
T256001

This old mansion was considerably improved and enlarged in 1785. It was the home of the Rt Hon Harbord Harbord, who was created Lord Suffield in 1786.

EX
4569
LAH 500

NORTH WALSHAM
The Market Cross
c1955 N42001

Bishop Thirlby built the market cross in the 16th century. It is an octagonal structure made of wood with an unusual three-tiered dome. The town took the cross over and installed a chimney clock in 1899. The library on the square (right) boasts that it is 'the largest in East Anglia'.

NORTH WALSHAM
The Pump c1955 N42035

This wonderful hand-operated water pump is on display under the market cross. It needed the strong iron-clad solid wooden wheels in order to travel over the cobbled streets of the town.

NORTH WALSHAM
Market Place c1955 N42022

North Walsham has a long history as a weaving town producing a lightweight cloth; there were also foundries here manufacturing farming machinery and implements, which were sold all over the area from farming shows. The buildings in the market place are typical three-storey houses with shops underneath. Most are family-owned, supplemented by more well-known names such as Boots (left). Lord Nelson was a pupil for three years at the town's Paston Grammar School.

WORSTEAD
A Weaver's Cottage c1955 W355011

This is a classic example of a weaver's cottage. The village is famous for being the centre of the worsted cloth trade. The manufacture of this material started in the 13th century and finished 600 years later. The skill of Flemish weavers who came to Norfolk was responsible for the enormous expansion of the trade.

◀ **STALHAM**
Hunsett Mill
c1955 S467056

This scene is worthy of a painting; it shows a typical windpump used to drain the reclaimed marshes. The reeds and rushes have grown high, and this area is famous for white water lilies, orchids and other flora which are in danger of extinction thanks to grazing animals. The family in the boat are enjoying sailing on a light breeze, and the boy on the bank is fishing, probably for tench, although eel catching is more popular.

SUTTON
The Sutton Windmill c1955
S473004

This huge nine-storey mill can be seen for miles. Built in 1859, it replaced another from the 1700s which burnt down. It had its own granary, and on the right we can see part of the miller's house, a very substantial building, so he must have been doing well. In this picture the mill looks forlorn without its sails, but it was restored to its full glory in 1976.

BACTON, *The Priory 1933* 85858

These are the ruins of Bromholm Priory, founded in 1113. It was famous for possessing 'the Holy Rood of Bromholm', said to be part of the true Cross. The village purchased it in 1223 and immediately miraculous cures began to happen, with dead people being restored to life. The same year Henry III visited the priory and granted the village a fair. There are interesting fragments of the priory remaining, particularly the transept, the chapter house and the dormitory.

MUNDESLEY
High Street 1921 71011

This is a very busy part of the village, which is not surprising - it was possible to purchase so many essential and varied items here. The thatched cottage was used by Spurgeon the butcher and then by Mace the cobbler; it is now a florist's. The other properties towards A R Steward's shop have been at various times a post office, a hardware store, and a chemist's. Arthur Steward was a draper, a shoe and boot retailer and a supplier of made-to-measure suits. The village was almost self-sufficient with these and other family-owned businesses.

MUNDESLEY, *The Sands 1892* 30639

Bathing machines, tents and cabins were rented out by George Johnson & Son until 1912. Storms in that year destroyed most of their equipment, and they were unable to afford replacements. After the 1914-18 war the local council took over and charged 6d for tents and cabins. For the princely sum of 5s, the bathing machines, which were mainly used by ladies, could be drawn right up to the water's edge by a horse. The gathering in the centre of the picture could be an orderly queue to purchase tea and coffee, sweets and other goods from stall holders, or maybe even to see and hear travelling musicians.

MUNDESLEY
Brooke Cottage 1921
71012

Brooke Cottage was the place to visit for parents and children alike if they had a sweet tooth, for it was formerly the village sweet shop and store. Next door there was a shoe shop and cobbler's. The dusty roads were regularly sprayed with water in the summer to protect walking pedestrians. Sometime after this picture was taken, the property was condemned and partly rebuilt using local flint.

MUNDESLEY, *The Beach Cafe c1955* M109046

This popular cafe supplied everything to provide a fun day for all the family: buckets, spades, fishing nets and trays of tea and sandwiches. What it did not supply was thermal swimwear, which accounts for the lack of swimmers in the sea. Owing to flooding and coastal erosion problems, the cafe was soon to be demolished and another built in its place on high stilts, together with improved sea defences to preserve this area of the beach.

CROMER AND THE NORTH COAST

OVERSTRAND
The Village 1906 56867

Dressed in all their finery, Mum and Dad are hoping to protect their daughter from the herd of cows coming towards them. There is very little grazing in this street apart from the gardens fronting the houses on the left - fortunately, the garden gates are all securely closed! The large building in the background is the popular Overstrand Hotel.

OVERSTRAND
The Sands 1906
56868

Overstrand is adjacent to Cromer. Its church disappeared from the cliffs into the ever-encroaching sea in the reign of Richard II. Another was built, and that too was a ruin for a number of years - it has since been restored. In this picture smart young men stroll along the beach, and ladies who are brave enough to enter the sea would change into their swimsuits in the bathing tents.

CROMER
From The West 1894
33322

By this time, Cromer had developed into a select holiday resort for the well-to-do, many of whom stayed in the Cliftonville Hotel (right) facing the west beach. The less well-off also caught the holiday bug; they were accommodated by the locals, who found they could make a bob of two by creating spare rooms, furnished sparsely but sufficiently well to put up 'to let' signs - perhaps this was the start of the seaside landlady tradition.

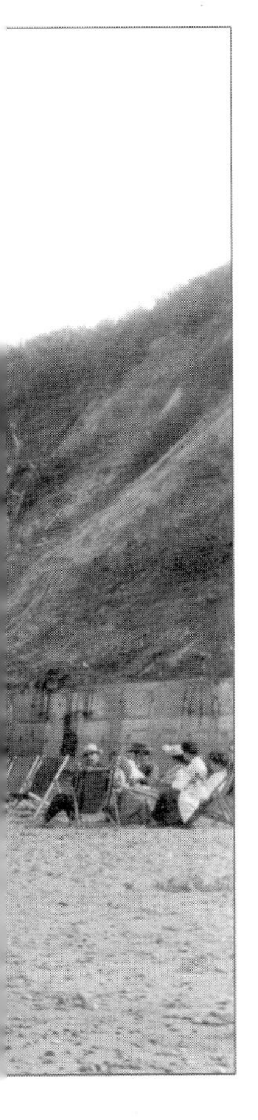

▲ **CROMER,** *The Garden of Sleep 1899* 44491

The gravestones belonged to St Michael's church, which was in Sidestrand. They are surrounded by poppies, which grew in profusion along this cliff top - it is now known as 'Poppyland'. You will not be able to see this tower again unless you own a wet suit and aqualung, for it slipped into the sea below in 1916.

◀ **CROMER**
The Sands 1906 56855

Boasting several large hotels, especially the Hotel de Paris which is right opposite the pier entrance, Cromer had become a very select place to visit. Personalities like Oscar Wilde, Shackleton, Einstein, Winston Churchill and members of European royal families came here, to name but a few. Ladies in their finery paraded on the promenade and jetty during the day and especially in the evenings. The picture shows a typical summer's day on east beach, with children building sandcastles or digging for creatures, treasures, or whatever their imagination desires.

JARROLD & SONS
POST OFFICE
POST OFFICE

CROMER
Church Street 1902
49071

By the time of this photograph Cromer had experienced a continuing building boom, which included new premises for fashionable stores such as Jarrold & Sons (left), who are still flourishing both in Cromer and Norwich. There were several attempts to promote the town as a spa, but the quality of the waters could not compare with Bath, Harrogate or Tunbridge Wells, so this never got off the ground. The church of St Peter and St Paul was built at the end of the 14th century and can hold a huge congregation. Children of the famous Gurney family (one of the founders of Barclays' Bank) stayed in lodgings in this street, on the site of the present Boots the chemist. A very stern Dr Fenner had his practice here in Hamilton House; he is reputed to have chastised a young Winston Churchill, who had badly misbehaved and injured his nanny in a tantrum.

CROMER, *The Cliffs 1925* 77511

Not only is the photographer on the cliff top taking a picture of his ladies with the lens into the sun, he is at great risk of losing his and their lives by going near the edge of these dangerous cliffs, which are constantly being eroded by the sea and the elements. This picture gives us a nice view of Cromer pier in the distance (left).

EAST RUNTON
The Beach Entrance 1921 70967

A leisured stroll on the cliff-top path leads to Cromer - otherwise rest awhile on the benches and admire the scenery and beach activities. Originally known as East Runton Gap, this area has been used by fishermen for centuries. There are dangerous currents for swimmers and boats, and there have been many shipwrecks here, which provided bounty for local inhabitants.

EAST RUNTON, *High Street c1955* E11040A

There are almost as many visitors in this High Street as there are in its neighbour Cromer, with every other premises a cafe or public house. The White Horse Inn dates from 1851, and was built on land owned by William Primrose, a brewer from Trunch. Another older pub, the Fishing Boat, dates from 1840. There is no pier here, but East Runton attracts people who prefer quieter beaches and country scenery.

▼ **EAST RUNTON,** *The Viaduct 1933* 85826

This five-span viaduct carries the Cromer to Holt railway line along huge embankments. The line was opened in 1887 and had an enormous impact on the village, creating a dramatic increase in house and shop building to accommodate the large numbers of visitors.

► **WEST RUNTON**
The Inn and the Sports Club 1938 88854

The inn was built in 1927 using traditional materials, especially local flint; its design makes it look much older then it really is. Before this date, and even in medieval times, the village had at least two ale houses. The inn has beautiful gardens, and a putting green. It is also the base where local cricket, darts and football teams meet. Being on the junction of the coast and beach road, it provides a convenient watering-hole for tourists.

WEST RUNTON
Beeston Priory 1894 33319

This ancient priory was founded around 1216 by Margaret Cressy. Apart from benefactions, the monks also received a share of the profits made from shipwrecks, and any other items of value which were washed ashore between Runton and Beeston.

WEST RUNTON
The Shops 1923
74219

These are few of the popular village shops which provide everything that the locals and visitors require. Only five minutes from the beach, they are on the coast road which used to be known as the King's Highway - this was a 15th-century common way or track to the local villages.

WEST RUNTON, *Pretty Corner 1925* 78707

These ladies are strolling on one of the highest hills in North Norfolk. Pretty Corner is aptly named, and the title applies to them as well as to the wonderful scenery visible from this point.

BEESTON REGIS
The Priory 1921
70996

Abbeys or priories in this area almost pale into insignificance when compared with nearby Walsingham. Lady Isabel de Cressey founded this priory for Augustinian canons in the reign of King John. It was merely a tranquil retreat for pilgrims, and like many others, the ruins over a time were incorporated into nearby farm buildings.

SHERINGHAM, *The Promenade 1906* 56877

The gentleman proudly escorts three elegant ladies dressed in white; other people further back are intrigued by the crab boats, which were probably made by Leonard Lown or his son Henry. They started business in the 1860s, and the number of boats made by this firm and another called Emery's ran into hundreds. The flag poles on the hill were used for gale warnings, signals for ships and flags for special occasions such as Royal birthdays. The local flint was used for good effect on the promenade garden wall in the foreground.

SHERINGHAM
Fishermen Mending Crab Pots 1906 56879

These wonderful characters are keeping their pots in good order; this was an essential job for the fishermen when not at sea. They used local oak and hazel. The pots are kept stable on the sea bed with a cast iron weight. Can you guess which one is 'Red Eye' West, 'Lotion Tar' Bishop or 'Bumshee' West? (They are the three in the centre). There was great rivalry between Cromer and Sheringham crabbers which often resulted in blows or the cutting of each others' ropes.

SHERINGHAM
The Sands 1921 70979

Note the boys in the centre. 'Yes', said Mother, 'you can play on the beach, but keep your shirt, tie and hat on - and your jacket'. Apart from this, most of the children in this picture are enjoying the delights of a typical English beach holiday. The beach huts are at a rakish angle, but are protected against the strong winds by the sea wall. The cliff pathway in the distance is the start of a scenic walk to Cromer, some three miles away.

▲ **SHERINGHAM**
High Street 1921 70993

The Mary Pym clock sits on top of the town's conduit, which had a trough for horses and a smaller one for dogs. The flint-faced buildings on the right are some of the original village houses, but virtually all the rest of the High Street buildings have been replaced. On the left of Rusts is another draper called Hunts, considered 'posh' by the locals; this nickname stuck to its owner Walter Hunt. Marches premises had several occupants, including Watsons Drapery and Craskes, who were famous Norfolk pork butchers.

► **SALTHOUSE**
The Creek c1955 S507010

Salt panning was an important industry in this area, and the output from Salthouse provided the local fishermen with all their needs. The salt marshes are famous for their varied wildlife. The ducks on this creek are well fed by motorists who stop to feed them from the coast road which runs in front of Bob Cooke's house (left), where he sold fresh bait and samphire, known as 'the poor man's asparagus'.

▲ **SALTHOUSE**
The Dun Cow c1955 S507033

This ancient public house stands on the edge of level salt marshes that run for miles along this part of the coast, which is known for wildfowl and other bird life. The village was once a seaport, and is scattered over a large area. It is hard to believe that it was once alive with dock workers, tradesmen and sailors. When the fens were reclaimed in the 17th century, the main sea channel became too shallow for boats to come in. The pub and other cottages have marks on their sides to indicate the height of the sea water which has flooded the area on several occasions.

◀ **CLEY NEXT THE SEA**
The Old Windmill c1955 C118002

The mill was built in the 1800s and continued to operate until 1921, when it and the maltings were converted into an unusual home. Like other interesting buildings in the area, it joined the holiday industry and became a guest house. Its image can be found on many calendars throughout the country.

▼ **HOLKHAM HALL** *1922* 72639

Holkham Hall was built in the 18th century by Thomas Coke, Earl of Leicester to a design by Palladio. The huge building is set in a park of over 3,000 acres, which on certain days in the summer are opened to the public. This picture shows the south front with its fine portico with an entablature supported by eight Corinthian columns. In front of it is a small covered stall set up for a local charitable event. Within the entrance hall are more beautiful columns and statues. One statue is of Diana, and is said to be one of the best examples of classical drapery in existence.

► **HOLT**
Holt Hall 1896 37987

This fine gabled building with huge chimneys is situated on the edge of the town, set in typical English parkland with lakes and rare trees. Its location prevented it from being damaged by a fire which demolished the town in the 17th century.

HOLT
The Methodist Free Church and the Milestone 1896 37982

The milestone is known to the locals as 'the pineapple'; it is inscribed with names and mileages from Holt to Norfolk's principal towns. The lamp post has been replaced by a more ornate lantern celebrating Queen Victoria's Jubilee. This was relocated from the market place, and the locals call it 'Blind Sam's Lamp'. The locals call themselves 'Holt Owls', but that's another story! In contrast to most other Wesleyan chapels, this Methodist Free Church is a grand building inside and out. The Norfolk architect Thomas Jeckyll used contrasting materials, which the Victorians adored; the building made a huge impact in the county when it was opened in April 1863. Its elaborate tower does not contain bells or anything else, apart from splendid accommodation for the local pigeons.

GLANDFORD
The Church 1896
37994

This church has been in ruins for years; it provided food and accommodation for many birds in its covering of ivy. However, this wildlife motel has been closed, for the church was completely restored four years after this picture was taken.

WALSINGHAM
The Old Pump 1922
72627

This old dome-shaped weather-beaten pump dates back to medieval times, and is situated at an important junction in the middle of this historic town. It has a fire beacon or brazier on top of its stone roof.

WALSINGHAM, *Old Houses 1929* 82031

This attractive small town has many picturesque old houses in its narrow streets. The village shop (centre) does a good trade in cycle parts, but at certain times in the religious calendar, pilgrims arrive on foot from all over Europe. A large number of religious houses exist, and there was an Augustinian priory here as far back as 1061. The half-timbered jettied building has a steep roof of cascading pantiles. On the right is the 60ft-high west gate to the once huge priory, which was surrounded by a high wall one mile long. Unfortunately, part of the wall near the gate has been converted into public toilets - although essential, they seem out of place.

WALSINGHAM, *The Black Lion Hotel 1929* 82033

This town is often over-run by pilgrims and tourists, but the local inhabitants still require basic essentials, even coal (left) and petrol for their vehicles (right). The Black Lion hotel is over 400 years old; although holy water is available from the spring in the shrine of Our Lady, even visiting clergy have been known to enjoy a chat over a glass of ale in this establishment. It was the most well-known non-monastic inn in Walsingham. Its construction is interesting, particularly the roof, which has a double queen-post structure.

◄ **BLAKENEY**
The Blakeney Hotel 1925 77525

Trading from its port ended in 1922, and this heralded the start of Blakeney as a tourist centre, specialising in boating, fishing, walking, painting, bird-watching and nature study. Costing £31,000 to build, the Blakeney Hotel (left) opened in 1923 with proud boasts of Mauretania-style heating stoves running on oil. High season rates were around seven guineas per person inclusive of four meals per day. For 3/6d extra, a guest could have a fire in their room every day. Visitors could have a splendid dinner for 5/6d. In this year the lifeboat 'Caroline' was taken out of service after twenty years of valiant rescues.

◄ **WALSINGHAM**
High Street 1933 85840

The long straight high street eventually opens up into the Friday market place. There are early 17th-century buildings here, which have been considerably altered over the centuries; these have had brick façades built over their front walls. A number of these houses have been converted into shops to cater for the visitors and pilgrims who flock to this town and visit the shrine of Our Lady of Walsingham.

▲ **WELLS-NEXT-THE-SEA,** *The Beach 1929* 81990

If there were coconut trees, you could well imagine this was a picture of a South Sea island. These colourful beach huts provide a place to change into swimwear or to have a welcome brew-up of tea. The extensive sandy beach is protected by a bank of sand which has a natural windbreak of high fir trees.

◄ **WELLS-NEXT-THE-SEA**
East End 1929 82001

The east end part of the quay faces northwards with views across the flat marshes to the sea beyond. The man in the boat has maybe rowed across to pick samphire from the muddy creeks; this is a local plant, a delicacy called 'poor mans asparagus'. In the 1920s this food was not well known in the larger central towns of Norfolk. Gales and floods have destroyed many old buildings in Wells, but there are still some early 17th-century flint and brick houses to be seen.

WELLS-NEXT-THE-SEA
The Quay c1955 W48064

The Great Eastern Railway Company developed the quayside, and freight trains rolled under the high platform of the tall granary warehouse to receive produce. Now only small coastal steamers are able to navigate the difficult channels to reach the quayside. The history and make-up of the town has dramatically changed over the years. From being a huge seaport, with a fishing industry which brought in the famous Wells whelks, it is now a popular spot for tourists. The sandy beach is about a mile from the quay, but if you are loaded down with picnic hampers and children, there is a small single-track steam train that will take you almost to the water's edge.

KING'S LYNN AND THE NORTH-WEST

HUNSTANTON
The Church 1896 38412

This church is located close to the entrance of the park surrounding Hunstanton Hall, which was built by Sir Roger L'Estrange in the 16th century; he was a writer who favoured the Royalist cause, and he founded the first real newspaper published in England. The church has tombs and fine brasses to the L'Estrange family; it also has a restored painted screen and a late Norman font.

HUNSTANTON
The Cross and the Green 1898 40898

This popular seaside town was built around a mill and an old village. The cliffs rise to about 70ft, and are the seaward end of the chalk ridge which stretches right across Norfolk. It is not as draughty here as it is on the east coast, but this photograph must have been taken on a cold day: all the visitors have moved inside the Golden Lion Hotel for refreshment, a quiet read, or a game of billiards. The Green is surrounded by good-quality hotels, and the local council selected this prestigious spot for the Town Hall (right).

HUNSTANTON, *The Pier 1901* 47646

The pier was built in 1870 and stretches 800ft into the sea. It was a focal point of this popular coastal resort, providing a short bracing walk over the briny and a welcome meal afterwards. Unfortunately, the pier was washed away during storms and gales in the 1970s.

HUNSTANTON
The Green and the Pier 1927 79723

What a scene this is, with bathers in the water, and gentlemen sitting on benches putting the world to rights. Tourists are ordering tickets for the twice-nightly end-of-the-pier show. Children are drinking from the outside fountain (right), and to top it all there is a horse-drawn ice cream cart. What has disappeared are the bathing machines, although the town still has a genteel air about it - Hunstanton must have been heaven to the regular visitors from the industrial North and Midlands. At the time of writing, this pier has been the victim of a massive fire.

WOLFERTON
The Station 1921
71063

Wolferton is the station nearest Sandringham. For nearly 50 years, trains brought royalty and statesmen from all over the world to this beautiful station. Even the lamps on the gate posts have royal crowns on top. Because of its importance, the locals take great pride in keeping the whole village maintained in an immaculate condition.

▲ **WOLFERTON,** *The Station 1921* 71064

This station would pass any CO's stringent inspection. It is built with many private rooms, some even oak-panelled, which provided the royal family and their guests with a quiet area to rest after their train journey before the arrival of their carriages from Sandringham. Shooting parties from the Royal Estate occasionally used the rooms for rest and refreshment.

◀ **SANDRINGHAM HOUSE** *1896* 38395

The royal family still enjoy their Christmas every year at Sandringham. Most of the family get together, and they can enjoy themselves in complete privacy in this their favourite retreat. This picture shows the east front of the house.

▲ **SANDRINGHAM**
The Entrance Lodge 1896 38401

Under this neatly-trimmed ivy and bushes is the entrance lodge to Sandringham House and gardens, which were subsequently opened to the public in the early 1900s.

► **SANDRINGHAM**
The Gardener's Cottage 1927 79758

This imposing cottage was for the important Head Gardener, who had over 80 gardeners under his control. The greenhouses provided most of the pot plants and flowers which were used in the house, and were used to cultivate roses, tomatoes and orchids. The public are not allowed into the cottage or this part of the estate.

▲ **SANDRINGHAM**
The Dutch Gardens and the Dairy 1927
79763

This property was built for Princess Alexandra; it is a similar design to the Swiss Cottage at Osborne House. The princess loved to entertain her friends here with tea and cakes, and butter and cheese made in the dairy from Danish cows which she had brought over from her homeland.

◄ **CASTLE RISING**
The Cross 1908 60033

This is constructed of Barnack stone, apart from the base, which came from the castle ruins. This is where regular market days were held, with farmers and traders selling all kinds of products, including small live stock.

CASTLE RISING, *The Castle 1898* 40894

Built on a large mound which was part of the town's defences, this is one of Britain's largest keeps. There is a well-preserved medieval kitchen, and the keep is richly decorated throughout.

KING'S LYNN, *Grey Friars Tower 1891* 28768

This tower escaped demolition during the Dissolution because it was a prominent landmark for ships entering the harbour. Originally it was the central tower of a Franciscan church with an unusual hexagonal design.

KING'S LYNN
Market Place 1898
40886

Since the 12th century, markets have been held on this cobbled square - it covers over 3 acres. It is surrounded by many important houses, some owned by the most wealthy merchants and families. Fairs, trials, and punishment were all carried out here, and witches were put in the stocks and sometimes boiled in oil.

KING'S LYNN
The Honest Lawyer Inn 1925 78717

The landlord is looking at our photographer with some suspicion, which is not surprising: this was thought to be one of Lynn's pubs with a dubious reputation. It makes you wonder why the pub sign depicts a lawyer with his decapitated head in his hand. A large number of pubs were closed when the licensing act of 1902 came into force.

DOWNHAM MARKET, *The Town Hall c1965* D149008

Built on a hill, Downham Market has extensive views over the River Ouse and the fens. It was a busy port, and its ancient market goes back to Edward the Confessor - it was celebrated for its Butter Market. Its buildings are varied and stylish, particularly those made of the local rust-coloured carr-stone. The Romans had a large settlement here.

CENTRAL NORFOLK

MELTON CONSTABLE
The Village 1922 72618

Children from the rather plain terraced houses have been given the job of taking the baby out for a pram ride. These buildings are in complete contrast to the home of Lord Hasting; the Hall has been a seat of the Astleys for centuries. The house is built of Norfolk brick with stone dressings, and is a fine example of Stuart design.

EAST BARSHAM
The Manor 1929 82045

This well-known manor house was built by Sir William Fermor during the reign of Henry VII. Other families who lived here were the Calthorpes and Le Stranges. The gatehouse has the arms of England and the ensigns of the Tudors and wonderful ornamental brickwork, with shields and medallions interspersed with the coats of arms of Henry of Lancaster and Elizabeth of York between Tudor roses. Henry VIII was a guest in 1511, and walked 2 miles barefoot to the shrine at Walsingham.

FAKENHAM, *Hempton Mill 1921* 71083

There is more than one way to catch a fish; onlookers must be amused at the antics of the unsuccessful fishermen. One in desperation has left his gear on the bank and has paddled into the river to assist the other hopefuls in an attempt to locate some fish. This large mill situated below the town on the river Wensum was built in 1833, and constructed of white brick and stone. It has an attractive ancient bridge of three arches; there is also a modern bridge on the right, which is less significant and made of wood.

▲ **FAKENHAM**

Market Place c1955 F3004

Markets have been held here on Thursdays for hundreds of years. They take place around the war memorial (left, in front of the white building); farmers, merchants and millers came from all areas of Norfolk. The Norfolk Chronicle newspaper had its headquarters here until 1955, when it was sold to ECN. The Crown Hotel (extreme left) is a popular spot for locals and visitors. The market place is surrounded by well-kept 18th-century buildings, but parking is a problem.

◄ **CASTLE ACRE**

The Priory, the West Front 1891 29113

This is one of Norfolk's most interesting and historic parishes. Situated on the Peddars Way on the banks of the River Nar, it has an old castle and a picturesque priory. William de Warrenne was granted Castle Acre by William the Conqueror. The Duke of Norfolk took it over after the Dissolution. Unfortunately, the castle and priory have been raided over the centuries to provide local building materials. This façade has beautiful arcading and mouldings. It is late Norman, apart from the large pointed window over the middle arch; on either side of this are two smaller arches which led to the north and south aisles. The priory occupied over 40 acres - there are remains of its flint boundary walls.

▼ SWAFFHAM, *Market Place 1891* 29103

King John granted markets here, and they have continued ever since. They take place around the Palladian-style market cross which is in the centre of five main roads. In the background is the tower of St Peter and St Paul's church, which has a fine hammer-beam roof with over 200 carved angels with shields. There are other carvings and rare books in the vestry. Swaffham's history is full of folk-lore, especially that of the Swaffham Tinker, who is depicted with his dogs in the church. The town is situated on one of Norfolk's rare hills, and some early houses had wells dug 105ft deep to obtain water.

▶ EAST DEREHAM
Market Place 1901 46546

This is the time when Dereham was in its prime. Its market was thriving and very active; this photograph was probably taken just before the arrival of the livestock - boys always made their extra pocket money helping the farmers and drovers control their animals. The square and its side streets are full of fine old houses and shops, along with exceptional Georgian properties. The rector of St Nicholas's church became Bishop Bonner of London in the 16th century. He was a ruthless man, and involved himself in sentencing wrong-doers to be burned at the stake - especially Protestants.

EAST DEREHAM
Market Place 1893
33304

This is the most central town in Norfolk. This view shows the varied façades of the buildings fronting the market place. The building next to the King's Arms Hotel on the right is a good example. Many of these ornate frontages were added by the Victorians especially to banks and hotels to give an improved image to customers. The Great Eastern Railway office (left) opened onto the market place near to the parcel receiving office. In the 16th century the town suffered two great fires, and the market place was greatly reduced in size following the rebuilding.

EAST DEREHAM
The County Schools 1893
33310

The town was fortunate to have a number of County Schools. The national school was attended by 200 boys and girls. The neat and commodious building was erected in 10 acres of land at a cost of £1,000, and received several endowments. When the railway reached East Dereham in 1882, the town's population increased, and another County School was opened. This was not successful, and was bought by the Watts Naval Training Organisation; the little lads in their sailors uniform were familiar sight in the town at weekends.

THETFORD AND THE SOUTH

THETFORD
The Grammar School 1921 70931

The school is a beautiful knapped flint and brick structure, and so is its surrounding wall; it was built in 1876. There have been important grammar schools in Thetford right back to 1566, when the Free Grammar School and hospital were founded by Sir Richard Fulmerton. One of its most famous pupils was the radical writer and activist Tom Paine, author of 'The Rights of Man' (1790-92). There is a statue of him in the town.

THETFORD
The Town Bridge
1929 81836

This neat cast iron bridge was built in 1829 replacing an old wooden bridge. It connects Norfolk to Suffolk over the River Ouse, making Thetford a border town.

MUNDFORD, *The Stores and the King's Head c1960* M310013

The pub and shop go back hundreds of years. This is a large village with a number of neat houses. It is close to the River Wissey and the main road to London. The village church is an ancient building with no tower, which is unusual for Norfolk.

▼ **EAST HARLING,** *High Street c1965* E132010

In the past there was a bustling livestock market and three annual fairs; the town was then known as Market Harling. It was already famous for the manufacture of linen and cloth. Its character changed in 1845 on the arrival of the railway when the population could easily travel to other towns and villages. The High Street still has shops, banks and pubs. Petty Sessions were held in the Swan Hotel, and the public house on the right has been a popular watering-hole since the early 1800s.

► **GARBOLDISHAM**
The Garage c1955
G188027

This small village is on the busy Diss to Thetford road. It has a number of attractive buildings of knapped flint - the garage is a prime example. The lorry driver is paying for his fuel, which has been dispensed from one of the huge petrol pumps.

HARLESTON
The Thoroughfare c1955 H305011

This small market town was named after a Danish leader called Herolveston. Harleston has retained its character, and has a good number of varied old buildings. The Magpie and the Swan Hotel are old coaching inns which are prominent amongst a mix of family-owned shops and businesses.

HINGHAM
Market Place c1955
H309014

These attractive 18th-century houses are good examples of houses which abound in this small town. A village sign by Harry Carter dominates the green. Hingham was responsible for providing New England with many settlers in the 17th century, where they founded another Hingham. Abraham Lincoln's ancestors came from here, and there is a bust of him in the aisle of the parish church.

WYMONDHAM
The Abbey 1891 29140

When they see it from the road or the nearby railway, travellers are puzzled by this church with towers at both ends. The church was part of a Benedictine abbey, originally a priory, founded by William d'Abini, Earl of Arundel in 1107. The ruin on the south-east of the church was the abbey's chapter house. Never fully completed, the west tower is 142ft 6ins high; the north porch has a groined roof with well-carved bosses. The nave has nine bays and a large triforium. Inside there are elaborate wood and stone carvings, a hammer-beam roof and a modern altar-screen, which is a war memorial.

WYMONDHAM, *The Market Place and the Cross c1965* W159035

This well-maintained timbered market cross was built in 1618. It provides a welcome resting place for shoppers and visitors. The modern shop fronts in the town hide many old medieval houses. Robert Kett, who led the rebellion in Norfolk during 1549, was born in Wymondham; he held the first meeting of peasants on Wymondham common.

INDEX

Frith Book Co Titles

www.francisfrith.co.uk

The Frith Book Company publishes over 100 new titles each year. A selection of those currently available are listed below. For latest catalogue please contact Frith Book Co.
Town Books 96 pages, approximately 100 photos. ***County and Themed Books*** 128 pages, approximately 150 photos (unless specified). All titles hardback with laminated case and jacket, except those indicated pb (paperback)

Title	ISBN	Price
Amersham, Chesham & Rickmansworth (pb)	1-85937-340-2	£9.99
Andover (pb)	1-85937-292-9	£9.99
Aylesbury (pb)	1-85937-227-9	£9.99
Barnstaple (pb)	1-85937-300-3	£9.99
Basildon Living Memories (pb)	1-85937-515-4	£9.99
Bath (pb)	1-85937-419-0	£9.99
Bedford (pb)	1-85937-205-8	£9.99
Bedfordshire Living Memories	1-85937-513-8	£14.99
Belfast (pb)	1-85937-303-8	£9.99
Berkshire (pb)	1-85937-191-4	£9.99
Berkshire Churches	1-85937-170-1	£17.99
Berkshire Living Memories	1-85937-332-1	£14.99
Black Country	1-85937-497-2	£12.99
Blackpool (pb)	1-85937-393-3	£9.99
Bognor Regis (pb)	1-85937-431-x	£9.99
Bournemouth (pb)	1-85937-545-6	£9.99
Bradford (pb)	1-85937-204-x	£9.99
Bridgend (pb)	1-85937-386-0	£7.99
Bridgwater (pb)	1-85937-305-4	£9.99
Bridport (pb)	1-85937-327-5	£9.99
Brighton (pb)	1-85937-192-2	£8.99
Bristol (pb)	1-85937-264-3	£9.99
British Life A Century Ago (pb)	1-85937-213-9	£9.99
Buckinghamshire (pb)	1-85937-200-7	£9.99
Camberley (pb)	1-85937-222-8	£9.99
Cambridge (pb)	1-85937-422-0	£9.99
Cambridgeshire (pb)	1-85937-420-4	£9.99
Cambridgeshire Villages	1-85937-523-5	£14.99
Canals And Waterways (pb)	1-85937-291-0	£9.99
Canterbury Cathedral (pb)	1-85937-179-5	£9.99
Cardiff (pb)	1-85937-093-4	£9.99
Carmarthenshire (pb)	1-85937-604-5	£9.99
Chelmsford (pb)	1-85937-310-0	£9.99
Cheltenham (pb)	1-85937-095-0	£9.99
Cheshire (pb)	1-85937-271-6	£9.99
Chester (pb)	1-85937-382 8	£9.99
Chesterfield (pb)	1-85937-378-x	£9.99
Chichester (pb)	1-85937-228-7	£9.99
Churches of East Cornwall (pb)	1-85937-249-x	£9.99
Churches of Hampshire (pb)	1-85937-207-4	£9.99
Cinque Ports & Two Ancient Towns	1-85937-492-1	£14.99
Colchester (pb)	1-85937-188-4	£8.99
Cornwall (pb)	1-85937-229-5	£9.99
Cornwall Living Memories	1-85937-248-1	£14.99
Cotswolds (pb)	1-85937-230-9	£9.99
Cotswolds Living Memories	1-85937-255-4	£14.99
County Durham (pb)	1-85937-398-4	£9.99
Croydon Living Memories (pb)	1-85937-162-0	£9.99
Cumbria (pb)	1-85937-621-5	£9.99
Derby (pb)	1-85937-367-4	£9.99
Derbyshire (pb)	1-85937-196-5	£9.99
Derbyshire Living Memories	1-85937-330-5	£14.99
Devon (pb)	1-85937-297-x	£9.99
Devon Churches (pb)	1-85937-250-3	£9.99
Dorchester (pb)	1-85937-307-0	£9.99
Dorset (pb)	1-85937-269-4	£9.99
Dorset Coast (pb)	1-85937-299-6	£9.99
Dorset Living Memories (pb)	1-85937-584-7	£9.99
Down the Severn (pb)	1-85937-560-x	£9.99
Down The Thames (pb)	1-85937-278-3	£9.99
Down the Trent	1-85937-311-9	£14.99
East Anglia (pb)	1-85937-265-1	£9.99
East Grinstead (pb)	1-85937-138-8	£9.99
East London	1-85937-080-2	£14.99
East Sussex (pb)	1-85937-606-1	£9.99
Eastbourne (pb)	1-85937-399-2	£9.99
Edinburgh (pb)	1-85937-193-0	£8.99
England In The 1880s	1-85937-331-3	£17.99
Essex - Second Selection	1-85937-456-5	£14.99
Essex (pb)	1-85937-270-8	£9.99
Essex Coast	1-85937-342-9	£14.99
Essex Living Memories	1-85937-490-5	£14.99
Exeter	1-85937-539-1	£9.99
Exmoor (pb)	1-85937-608-8	£9.99
Falmouth (pb)	1-85937-594-4	£9.99
Folkestone (pb)	1-85937-124-8	£9.99
Frome (pb)	1-85937-317-8	£9.99
Glamorgan	1-85937-488-3	£14.99
Glasgow (pb)	1-85937-190-6	£9.99
Glastonbury (pb)	1-85937-338-0	£7.99
Gloucester (pb)	1-85937-232-5	£9.99
Gloucestershire (pb)	1-85937-561-8	£9.99
Great Yarmouth (pb)	1-85937-426-3	£9.99
Greater Manchester (pb)	1-85937-266-x	£9.99
Guildford (pb)	1-85937-410-7	£9.99
Hampshire (pb)	1-85937-279-1	£9.99
Harrogate (pb)	1-85937-423-9	£9.99
Hastings and Bexhill (pb)	1-85937-131-0	£9.99
Heart of Lancashire (pb)	1-85937-197-3	£9.99
Helston (pb)	1-85937-214-7	£9.99
Hereford (pb)	1-85937-175-2	£9.99
Herefordshire (pb)	1-85937-567-7	£9.99
Herefordshire Living Memories	1-85937-514-6	£14.99
Hertfordshire (pb)	1-85937-247-3	£9.99
Horsham (pb)	1-85937-432-8	£9.99
Humberside (pb)	1-85937-605-3	£9.99
Hythe, Romney Marsh, Ashford (pb)	1-85937-256-2	£9.99
Ipswich (pb)	1-85937-424-7	£9.99
Isle of Man (pb)	1-85937-268-6	£9.99
Isle of Wight (pb)	1-85937-429-8	£9.99
Isle of Wight Living Memories	1-85937-304-6	£14.99
Kent (pb)	1-85937-189-2	£9.99
Kent Living Memories(pb)	1-85937-401-8	£9.99
Kings Lynn (pb)	1-85937-334-8	£9.99

Available from your local bookshop or from the publisher

Frith Book Co Titles (continued)

Lake District (pb)	1-85937-275-9	£9.99
Lancashire Living Memories	1-85937-335-6	£14.99
Lancaster, Morecambe, Heysham (pb)	1-85937-233-3	£9.99
Leeds (pb)	1-85937-202-3	£9.99
Leicester (pb)	1-85937-381-x	£9.99
Leicestershire & Rutland Living Memories	1-85937-500-6	£12.99
Leicestershire (pb)	1-85937-185-x	£9.99
Lighthouses	1-85937-257-0	£9.99
Lincoln (pb)	1-85937-380-1	£9.99
Lincolnshire (pb)	1-85937-433-6	£9.99
Liverpool and Merseyside (pb)	1-85937-234-1	£9.99
London (pb)	1-85937-183-3	£9.99
London Living Memories	1-85937-454-9	£14.99
Ludlow (pb)	1-85937-176-0	£9.99
Luton (pb)	1-85937-235-x	£9.99
Maidenhead (pb)	1-85937-339-9	£9.99
Maidstone (pb)	1-85937-391-7	£9.99
Manchester (pb)	1-85937-198-1	£9.99
Marlborough (pb)	1-85937-336-4	£9.99
Middlesex	1-85937-158-2	£14.99
Monmouthshire	1-85937-532-4	£14.99
New Forest (pb)	1-85937-390-9	£9.99
Newark (pb)	1-85937-366-6	£9.99
Newport, Wales (pb)	1-85937-258-9	£9.99
Newquay (pb)	1-85937-421-2	£9.99
Norfolk (pb)	1-85937-195-7	£9.99
Norfolk Broads	1-85937-486-7	£14.99
Norfolk Living Memories (pb)	1-85937-402-6	£9.99
North Buckinghamshire	1-85937-626-6	£14.99
North Devon Living Memories	1-85937-261-9	£14.99
North Hertfordshire	1-85937-547-2	£14.99
North London (pb)	1-85937-403-4	£9.99
North Somerset	1-85937-302-x	£14.99
North Wales (pb)	1-85937-298-8	£9.99
North Yorkshire (pb)	1-85937-236-8	£9.99
Northamptonshire Living Memories	1-85937-529-4	£14.99
Northamptonshire	1-85937-150-7	£14.99
Northumberland Tyne & Wear (pb)	1-85937-281-3	£9.99
Northumberland	1-85937-522-7	£14.99
Norwich (pb)	1-85937-194-9	£8.99
Nottingham (pb)	1-85937-324-0	£9.99
Nottinghamshire (pb)	1-85937-187-6	£9.99
Oxford (pb)	1-85937-411-5	£9.99
Oxfordshire (pb)	1-85937-430-1	£9.99
Oxfordshire Living Memories	1-85937-525-1	£14.99
Paignton (pb)	1-85937-374-7	£7.99
Peak District (pb)	1-85937-280-5	£9.99
Pembrokeshire	1-85937-262-7	£14.99
Penzance (pb)	1-85937-595-2	£9.99
Peterborough (pb)	1-85937-219-8	£9.99
Picturesque Harbours	1-85937-208-2	£14.99
Piers	1-85937-237-6	£17.99
Plymouth (pb)	1-85937-389-5	£9.99
Poole & Sandbanks (pb)	1-85937-251-1	£9.99
Preston (pb)	1-85937-212-0	£9.99
Reading (pb)	1-85937-238-4	£9.99
Redhill to Reigate (pb)	1-85937-596-0	£9.99
Ringwood (pb)	1-85937-384-4	£7.99
Romford (pb)	1-85937-319-4	£9.99
Royal Tunbridge Wells (pb)	1-85937-504-9	£9.99
Salisbury (pb)	1-85937-239-2	£9.99
Scarborough (pb)	1-85937-379-8	£9.99
Sevenoaks and Tonbridge (pb)	1-85937-392-5	£9.99
Sheffield & South Yorks (pb)	1-85937-267-8	£9.99
Sherborne (pb)	1-85937-301-1	£9.99
Shrewsbury (pb)	1-85937-325-9	£9.99
Shropshire (pb)	1-85937-326-7	£9.99
Shropshire Living Memories	1-85937-643-6	£14.99
Somerset	1-85937-153-1	£14.99
South Devon Coast	1-85937-107-8	£14.99
South Devon Living Memories (pb)	1-85937-609-6	£9.99
South East London (pb)	1-85937-263-5	£9.99
South Somerset	1-85937-318-6	£14.99
South Wales	1-85937-519-7	£14.99
Southampton (pb)	1-85937-427-1	£9.99
Southend (pb)	1-85937-313-5	£9.99
Southport (pb)	1-85937-425-5	£9.99
St Albans (pb)	1-85937-341-0	£9.99
St Ives (pb)	1-85937-415-8	£9.99
Stafford Living Memories (pb)	1-85937-503-0	£9.99
Staffordshire (pb)	1-85937-308-9	£9.99
Stourbridge (pb)	1-85937-530-8	£9.99
Stratford upon Avon (pb)	1-85937-388-7	£9.99
Suffolk (pb)	1-85937-221-x	£9.99
Suffolk Coast (pb)	1-85937-610-x	£9.99
Surrey (pb)	1-85937-240-6	£9.99
Surrey Living Memories	1-85937-328-3	£14.99
Sussex (pb)	1-85937-184-1	£9.99
Sutton (pb)	1-85937-337-2	£9.99
Swansea (pb)	1-85937-167-1	£9.99
Taunton (pb)	1-85937-314-3	£9.99
Tees Valley & Cleveland (pb)	1-85937-623-1	£9.99
Teignmouth (pb)	1-85937-370-4	£7.99
Thanet (pb)	1-85937-116-7	£9.99
Tiverton (pb)	1-85937-178-7	£9.99
Torbay (pb)	1-85937-597-9	£9.99
Truro (pb)	1-85937-598-7	£9.99
Victorian & Edwardian Dorset	1-85937-254-6	£14.99
Victorian & Edwardian Kent (pb)	1-85937-624-X	£9.99
Victorian & Edwardian Maritime Album (pb)	1-85937-622-3	£9.99
Victorian and Edwardian Sussex (pb)	1-85937-625-8	£9.99
Villages of Devon (pb)	1-85937-293-7	£9.99
Villages of Kent (pb)	1-85937-294-5	£9.99
Villages of Sussex (pb)	1-85937-295-3	£9.99
Warrington (pb)	1-85937-507-3	£9.99
Warwick (pb)	1-85937-518-9	£9.99
Warwickshire (pb)	1-85937-203-1	£9.99
Welsh Castles (pb)	1-85937-322-4	£9.99
West Midlands (pb)	1-85937-289-9	£9.99
West Sussex (pb)	1-85937-607-x	£9.99
West Yorkshire (pb)	1-85937-201-5	£9.99
Weston Super Mare (pb)	1-85937-306-2	£9.99
Weymouth (pb)	1-85937-209-0	£9.99
Wiltshire (pb)	1-85937-277-5	£9.99
Wiltshire Churches (pb)	1-85937-171-x	£9.99
Wiltshire Living Memories (pb)	1-85937-396-8	£9.99
Winchester (pb)	1-85937-428-x	£9.99
Windsor (pb)	1-85937-333-x	£9.99
Wokingham & Bracknell (pb)	1-85937-329-1	£9.99
Woodbridge (pb)	1-85937-498-0	£9.99
Worcester (pb)	1-85937-165-5	£9.99
Worcestershire Living Memories	1-85937-489-1	£14.99
Worcestershire	1-85937-152-3	£14.99
York (pb)	1-85937-199-x	£9.99
Yorkshire (pb)	1-85937-186-8	£9.99
Yorkshire Coastal Memories	1-85937-506-5	£14.99
Yorkshire Dales	1-85937-502-2	£14.99
Yorkshire Living Memories (pb)	1-85937-397-6	£9.99

See Frith books on the internet at www.francisfrith.co.uk

FRITH PRODUCTS & SERVICES

Francis Frith would doubtless be pleased to know that the pioneering publishing venture he started in 1860 still continues today. Over a hundred and forty years later, The Francis Frith Collection continues in the same innovative tradition and is now one of the foremost publishers of vintage photographs in the world. Some of the current activities include:

Interior Decoration

Today Frith's photographs can be seen framed and as giant wall murals in thousands of pubs, restaurants, hotels, banks, retail stores and other public buildings throughout the country. In every case they enhance the unique local atmosphere of the places they depict and provide reminders of gentler days in an increasingly busy and frenetic world.

Product Promotions

Frith products are used by many major companies to promote the sales of their own products or to reinforce their own history and heritage. Frith promotions have been used by Hovis bread, Courage beers, Scots Porage Oats, Colman's mustard, Cadbury's foods, Mellow Birds coffee, Dunhill pipe tobacco, Guinness, and Bulmer's Cider.

Genealogy and Family History

As the interest in family history and roots grows world-wide, more and more people are turning to Frith's photographs of Great Britain for images of the towns, villages and streets where their ancestors lived; and, of course, photographs of the churches and chapels where their ancestors were christened, married and buried are an essential part of every genealogy tree and family album.

Frith Products

All Frith photographs are available Framed or just as Mounted Prints and Posters (size 23 x 16 inches). These may be ordered from the address below. From time to time other products - Address Books, Calendars, Table Mats, etc - are available.

The Internet

Already fifty thousand Frith photographs can be viewed and purchased on the internet through the Frith websites and a myriad of partner sites.

For more detailed information on Frith companies and products, look at these sites:

www.francisfrith.co.uk
www.francisfrith.com
(for North American visitors)

See the complete list of Frith Books at:
www.francisfrith.co.uk

This web site is regularly updated with the latest list of publications from the Frith Book Company. If you wish to buy books relating to another part of the country that your local bookshop does not stock, you may purchase on-line.

For further information, trade, or author enquiries please contact us at the address below:
The Francis Frith Collection, Frith's Barn, Teffont, Salisbury, Wiltshire, England SP3 5QP.
Tel: +44 (0)1722 716 376 Fax: +44 (0)1722 716 881 Email: sales@francisfrith.co.uk

See Frith books on the internet at www.francisfrith.co.uk

HOW TO ORDER YOUR FREE MOUNTED PRINT

and other Frith prints at half price

Mounted Print
Overall size 14 x 11 inches

Fill in and cut out this voucher and return it with your remittance for £2.25 (to cover postage and handling to UK addresses). For overseas addresses please include £4.00 post and handling. Choose any photograph included in this book. Your SEPIA print will be A4 in size. It will be mounted in a cream mount with a burgundy rule line (overall size 14 x 11 inches).

Order additional Mounted Prints at HALF PRICE (only £7.49 each*)
If you would like to order more Frith prints from this book, possibly as gifts for friends and family, you can buy them at half price (with no additional postage and handling costs).

Have your Mounted Prints framed
For an extra £14.95 per print* you can have your mounted print(s) framed in an elegant polished wood and gilt moulding, overall size 16 x 13 inches (no additional postage and handling required).

*** IMPORTANT!**

These special prices are only available if you order at the same time as you order your free mounted print. You must use the ORIGINAL VOUCHER on this page (no copies permitted). We can only despatch to one address.

Voucher *for **FREE** and Reduced Price Frith Prints*

Please do not photocopy this voucher. Only the original is valid, so please fill it in, cut it out and return it to us with your order.

Picture ref no	Page number	Qty	Mounted @ £7.49	Framed + £14.95	Total Cost
		1	Free of charge*	£	£
			£7.49	£	£
			£7.49	£	£
			£7.49	£	£
			£7.49	£	£
			£7.49	£	£

Please allow 28 days for delivery

* Post & handling (UK)	£3.50
Total Order Cost	£

Title of this book ....

I enclose a cheque/postal order for £ ....
made payable to 'The Francis Frith Collection'

OR please debit my Mastercard / Visa / Switch / Amex card
(credit cards please on all overseas orders), details below

Card Number

Issue No (Switch only) Valid from (Amex/Switch)

Expires Signature

Name Mr/Mrs/Ms ....

Address ....

....

....

.... Postcode ....

Daytime Tel No ....

Email ....

Valid to 31/12/05

Send completed Voucher form to:
The Francis Frith Collection, Frith's Barn, Teffont, Salisbury, Wiltshire SP3 5QP

Free Print - see overleaf

Would you like to find out more about Francis Frith?

We have recently recruited some entertaining speakers who are happy to visit local groups, clubs and societies to give an illustrated talk documenting Frith's travels and photographs. If you are a member of such a group and are interested in hosting a presentation, we would love to hear from you.

Our speakers bring with them a small selection of our local town and county books, together with sample prints. They are happy to take orders. A small proportion of the order value is donated to the group who have hosted the presentation. The talks are therefore an excellent way of fundraising for small groups and societies.

Can you help us with information about any of the Frith photographs in this book?

We are gradually compiling an historical record for each of the photographs in the Frith archive. It is always fascinating to find out the names of the people shown in the pictures, as well as insights into the shops, buildings and other features depicted.

If you recognize anyone in the photographs in this book, or if you have information not already included in the author's caption, do let us know. We would love to hear from you, and will try to publish it in future books or articles.

Our production team

Frith books are produced by a small dedicated team at offices in the converted Grade II listed 18th-century barn at Teffont near Salisbury, illustrated above. Most have worked with the Frith Collection for many years. All have in common one quality: they have a passion for the Frith Collection. The team is constantly expanding, but currently includes:

Jason Buck, John Buck, Douglas Burns, Ruth Butler, Heather Crisp, Isobel Hall, Hazel Heaton, Peter Horne, James Kinnear, Tina Leary, Sue Molloy, Hannah Marsh, Kate Rotondetto, Dean Scource, Eliza Sackett, Terence Sackett, Sandra Sanger, Lewis Taylor, and Shelley Tolcher.